"A Free Woman on God's Earth"

The True Story of
Elizabeth "Mumbet" Freeman,
The Slave Who Won Her Freedom

By

JANA LAIZ

&

ANN-ELIZABETH BARNES

Illustrated by JACQUELINE ROGERS

Crow Flies Press
The Berkshires, Massachusetts

Published by Crow Flies Press

Copyright © 2009 by Jana Laiz and Ann-Elizabeth Barnes
ISBN-9780981491028

Library of Congress Control Number: 2009936014

Visit us on the Web! www.crowfliespress.com

Printed in the United States

"Any time, any time when I was a slave,

if I had been offered one minute's freedom and told

that at the end of that minute

I would have to die, I would have taken it,

just to stand one minute

a free woman on God's earth,

I would."

Elizabeth "Mumbet" Freeman

ALSO BY JANA LAIZ

Weeping Under This Same Moon
Elephants of the Tsunami
The Twelfth Stone (coming soon)

Dedication

To my dear friend Ann-Elizabeth, who embodies the indomitable spirit of Mumbet and without whose knowledge and passion for our subject, unbridled humor and enthusiasm during the entire writing process, steadfast commitment to our project, and unwavering friendship, this book could never have been written.
JL

I dedicate this book to the abiding spirit of Mumbet. Since the day I first heard her story she has remained an inspiration to me in every aspect of my life. Her courage, her grace, her loving heart encouraged me to begin to spread my wings and feel that anything is possible. And to Jana, without whom none of this would have happened. And all my love and gratitude to my husband, Richard, who encourages and supports me in every project I undertake.
AE

For Rosie with love,
JR

PROLOGUE

1751

On a cool spring morning early in the
month of May a horse and cart clip-clopped
along the dirt road towards the quiet little
town of Sheffield, in the Berkshire Hills of
Massachusetts. The horse slowed as she spied
a stand of delicate grass along the roadside,
her lips quivering, ready to taste the sweet

1

clover. The driver pulled her head up harshly.

"Git on!" the man yelled, clucking his tongue for the horse to move. The horse obeyed her master and hurried on.

In the cart were gifts: gifts for Colonel John Ashley and his family. They were from Mrs. Ashley's father, Pieter Hogeboom, a wealthy Dutch merchant from the nearby town of Claverack in the state of New York. There were household goods for the kitchen, furniture for the parlor, two woolen rugs and three people: one man, one woman and one child. They were slaves. A slave was a person who did not get paid for work and was forced to do whatever they were told. Slaves were bought and sold, owned by another person, like an ox or a table. Men, women, even children were slaves. They had no rights, they could not give their opinion, nor were they free to make decisions on their own. They had to obey their master and mistress in all things.

These three sat quietly in the back of the wagon, stuck uncomfortably between chairs

and dishes. The child, a seven-year-old girl, sat sobbing, holding tightly to the woman who was not her mother. Her other hand clutched the flowered shawl that her own mother had given her before they took her away. It was wet with tears. She thought about her dear mother and the conversation they had had only a few hours before.

"Here, my sweet child, wrap this shawl around your shoulders," the girl's mother had said, putting the shawl over her and pulling her close. "And take this red petticoat and put it on under your shift."

"Why, Mama? Where am I going?" she recalled asking, fearful to know.

Her mother had taken her into her arms and held her tightly.

"Listen to me child, listen."

She had nodded quickly—her eyes wide with fear.

"You're going on a trip with Selah and John—I'm not sure where, but I believe you're going all the way to Massachusetts." She paused, and then, holding back her tears, tightening her grip on her daughter, she said slowly, "You won't be coming back."

The little girl in the cart squeezed her eyes shut as she remembered what had come next. Her mother had spoken in their familiar Dutch dialect.

"Don't be afraid, my dear one. Carry me with you in your heart—call for me when you feel afraid and I will come in spirit."

She had begun to tremble. What was happening? Why must she leave her family?

She put her small arms around her mother's waist.

"Oh Mama, please, I don't want to go! Please Mama, can't you do something?" But her mother only held her tighter, shaking her head back and forth.

"Oh child, Master Hogeboom is giving you to his daughter as a gift." She let go a sob. "I cannot stop this." She handed her daughter another piece of clothing, a cap for her head and a small leather bag.

"Don't forget what I have taught you. Keep yourself healthy with the herbs in this sack. Remember to look at the evening star every night and I will be there with you."

The little girl was stunned. She began to weep uncontrollably, hanging on to her mother's skirt. The two held each other as Selah came up the path with a grim look on her face. She enfolded the two of them into her own embrace and then, looking into the distraught mother's eyes, took the child from her and carried her to the waiting cart. The older slave had to hold tightly as the small child

7

struggled to run back to her mother. Just as Selah was about to place her into the cart, the girl saw her father hurrying up the road from the barley field. Her heart leapt with hope as she escaped from Selah's grasp.

"Oh, Papa, Papa, they're sending me away! Can't you do something?"

Her father, breathing hard, folded her into his big, strong arms and held her close for several long moments. Setting her down again, he took her face into his trembling hands and looked deeply her into her eyes. His own were filled with anguish.

"You must go, daughter, but I will be coming by at the end of August to pick up the harvest from Master Ashley. I will see you then!"

"But, Papa, why must I go? Why can I not stay here?"

"We are slaves. You know I cannot stop the Master."

She looked away, unable to meet her father's eyes. How could they let her go?

The little girl looked straight ahead as the cart rumbled along. She hiccupped, and tightened her grip on Selah's hand. Selah put her arm around her.

"Oh child, I will keep your mother and father in my heart, too, and we can tell each other our lovingest thoughts."

The little girl straightened her shoulders. She knew how to put on a brave face. Hadn't she done that many times before when Mistress Hogeboom had threatened her with punishment?

She smoothed out her dress and saw the red petticoat peeking out from underneath. She sighed, letting fresh tears escape and wrapped her shawl more tightly about her. She would always keep these treasures her mother had given her. She looked steadfastly ahead as the cart rumbled along the Albany Pike towards her new home.

The little girl in the cart was called Bet. This is her story.

Chapter 1

The year was 1751 and there were slaves then, even in Massachusetts. Being a slave often meant not having enough to eat, or warm clothes to wear, or enough sleep. Some slaves were beaten. The consequences of not doing what one was told to do were often unbearable.

Although the country had been home to the Native people for thousands of years, to the colonists it was wild and new. The land was filled with trees in an endless forest as far as the eye could see. The nearby hills teemed with bears, wolves, foxes and mountain lions. The sky was filled with birds. Fish were abundant in clear swift streams. To the settlers it seemed a howling wilderness. They had arrived in Sheffield only twenty-five years earlier. Forests had been cleared to build houses and plant crops.

Life was hard. Everyone had to work. Fathers and mothers, grandparents and children all had chores. Everyone had to share in the daily tasks, and there was much work to be done. Crops had to be planted and harvested, wood chopped, clothing woven and sewn, animals fed and milked, gardens tended. Some families had servants to help out, and others had slaves.

Colonel Ashley was an important man in the town of Sheffield. He was a lawyer, a judge, a farmer and landowner. He and Mrs. Ashley had four children— John, Mary, Jane and Hannah. They had a few

servants but he needed more help. His father-in-law was a wealthy man and sent him the three slaves as a gift for the family. They would do the work now. The little girl, Bet, who arrived that cool May morning, was expected to take on many household chores, working throughout the day.

Bet's first months at her new "home" seemed endless. Each day brought new chores, new things to learn, and new challenges to overcome. She longed to play with the other children, but Mrs. Ashley would not allow her to play for even a minute.

"Bet! Come here now and get this hearth clean. I don't want to see a speck of ash! Do you understand?" Mrs. Ashley commanded.

"Yes, ma'am." Bet not only swept the hearth, she collected kindling for the fires that warmed the house; she carried water and made the beds. She often looked to the Ashley girls for understanding but they took no notice of her.

"Bet! This bed isn't tight enough. Come and make it again!" Bet sighed, but knew she had no choice but to listen to the mistress. Punishment was not uncommon in the Ashley household.

"Bet! Fetch the eggs and hurry! And then get the water for the washing, and mind you don't dally by the river! There's more work to be done. Come to me in the parlor when you are finished."

"Yes, ma'am."

She wished she could join the Ashley children in their studies. Her mind and spirit yearned for knowledge. The days were long and hard. Her arms ached from chopping wood and carrying water and she was tired of building fires in the house's many fireplaces.

There were a few bright moments that help lift her spirits.

"C'mere child, come and help me with this bakin'," called Selah, seeing that Bet had finished drawing the water from the well.

"Coming Selah!" Bet called. Selah was now the closest thing Bet had to a mother. Bet ran to her and the woman patted her on her head. Bet would have liked to hug the older woman, but there was work to be done.

"Fetch me some rosemary for this bread," Selah said, winking at the young child. She knew that Bet was happy to do this, for her favorite place was in the garden among the herbs and flowers. Often, after

weeding the family's main garden, she rambled in the woods and collected wild herbs in a basket she had made. Before she had been enslaved to the Ashley family, Bet's mother had taught her which plants were for eating, and which were for healing. Collecting them always made her feel closer to her mother. Selah was a good teacher too. She taught Bet how to recognize and use the medicinal plants that grew alongside the kitchen herbs and in the woods.

Bet lingered for a moment in the garden taking in the fragrant smells. She watched the honeybees buzzing from flower to flower, collecting pollen. She lifted her face to the sun, letting its rays warm her. Then, knowing she had to help bake bread for the family's table, she reluctantly plucked the rosemary and returned to the kitchen. Tomorrow she would make candles for the family's lights and help with the hazardous task of making soap for their baths and washing up. Bet dreaded this task the most because she knew that she would have to stir the dangerous lye in the large kettle outside, making sure no lumps spoiled the fine soap. It was a weary life for a young girl. But Bet was a slave, so even if she was exhausted, she had to complete her tasks before she was allowed to rest. She couldn't go to her small bed until all the work was done, and she had to rise before the sun came up.

Chapter 2

The morning mist from the Housatonic River
swirled around Bet's ankles as she carried two
buckets of water up the steps to the house. Winter
seemed to be settling into the valley. Several years
had gone by and five slaves now lived on the Ashley
Farm. They slept in a small outbuilding set apart
from the main house. Bet liked to sing songs

quietly after dark with Selah and the other slaves—
John, Zack and Harry. It made her feel as though
she had a family. Selah and the older slaves tried
to do their best to care for her, but they could not
replace her real mother or father. Bet's father, as
promised, had come at the end of that first long
hard summer. Selah had arranged for Bet to
work in the fields that day, helping with the
harvest and so she was able to spend a few
precious hours with him. He had even stayed
the night, and they sang together and he told
her news from home and gave her more herbs
from her mother.

On starlit nights, Bet liked to look up at her
mother's star and hold her in her heart.

Bet often daydreamed of having a friend.
She realized that the Ashley children were
privileged but she could not understand why
they would not play with her. She wondered
what made her different.

"Selah, why am I not allowed to play with Jane and Mary? Why won't the mistress let me play when all my work is done?"

Selah looked at her sharply. "Child, you know why. We've spoke of this before. You're too big to ask me such questions."

"But..."

"Bet, I know you don't like to hear this but I am going to say it again – because our skin is black and theirs is white, we are slaves. This is how it is. We can't help it, but we have to accept it. Now, go fetch me the linen."

Bet heaved a sigh and went to the clothesline. She might not be able to do anything about it, but she wasn't going to accept it in her heart! Not for a minute!

Bet grew tall and strong. Before long she was half a head taller than Selah. Keeping herself tidy was important to her. Although Mrs. Ashley kept her working from morning until night, she always tried to keep her apron clean, her hair tucked neatly in her cap, her stockings mended. Doing the household tasks well gave her a sense of pride, especially her cooking. Under Selah's guidance, she became a very good cook and the whole household looked forward to her meals.

"What will you cook for supper tonight, Bet?" Colonel Ashley asked.

"Sir, what would you like?"

"I like anything you prepare, Bet."

"Thank you, sir. The mistress has ordered beef stew in a crock, red cabbage and apples with Cheddar biscuits on the side, and to top it off, vinegar pie."

"Ah, vinegar pie will hit the spot! I look forward to dinner, Bet."

Bet smiled, wishing her mistress could be as pleasant as the Colonel, but the mistress could never be pleased.

"Bet! These vegetables are overcooked!" Bet knew this was not so, but she had to apologize

just the same.

"Hannah, dear, they taste just fine to me," the Colonel said.

Mrs. Ashley glared at her husband. The children glared at their father. Colonel Ashley should know better than to cross his wife. And she would remind him that the slaves were a gift from *her* father. This made them more hers than his.

The Colonel sighed and ate his meal in silence.

ℰꝂ ℭℛ

"Bet," Mrs. Ashley called loudly out the door, "Bet!"

She looked about impatiently. Where was Bet, this girl who dared have a mind of her own? She would have to make her listen, break her independence, show her who was the mistress and who was the slave.

Bet appeared around the corner of the house, clutching her bonnet and a bouquet of wild flowers. "Here I am."

"Did I not request that you take this bottle of ale to my son's house?"

"I'm sorry! I was going to give the bottle of ale to Brom, who is here on an errand for your son, but Mrs. Root sent her servant round for bee balm for her foot and I was just fetching it."

Mrs. Ashley snorted. She only reluctantly allowed Bet to act as nursemaid to her neighbors and other church-going families. Why hadn't she prevented it years ago when Bet first showed skill as a healer? For Goodness sakes, couldn't her neighbors find their own cures for their silly ailments? After all, Bet was *her* slave, not everyone else's! thought Mrs. Ashley to herself.

Angrily, she handed Bet the bottle of ale and said, "Give it to Brom first, then do your business quickly. I have a long list of tasks that need doing."

Chapter 3

As Bet grew to be a young woman, Mrs. Ashley began relying on her for the smooth running of the household. Although the mistress didn't like to admit it, she knew that because of Bet, the house was always bright and warm, the meals prepared on time, the larder plentiful with vegetables from the garden, and the silver polished to a sheen. And though Bet ran the household better than her mistress, a kind word never crossed Mrs. Ashley's lips.

When Bet was in her mid-twenties she married a young man, a fellow slave, who lived nearby in another household. Although they

were married, Bet had to stay on the Ashley farm and couldn't live with her husband down the road. The Colonel did not allow the sharing of households. In spite of that, Bet grew in happiness. She spent as much time with her husband as possible. Sundays and evenings were their time together. Before long, they had a child, and they called her Little Bet. Bet delighted in teaching her the things she knew and loved.

"Little Bet, come here, put your nose in this bouquet! Do you know what it is?"

"Yes, Mama, lavender!"

"Well, pick some for Mrs. Root. She is making soap and needs a sweet smelling herb." Little Bet knew which herb to pick and did as she was asked.

With Little Bet always by her side, Bet began to be known affectionately as "Mumbet," perhaps because she deserved the title, "ma'am," perhaps also because she took care of so many of Mrs. Ashley's neighbors when they were sick. By contrast, people in town called Mrs. Ashley a "harridan" and a "shrew" because of her uncontrollable temper. The slaves and servants were afraid of her. All except Mumbet. She often protected them from Mrs. Ashley's angry tirades. She knew how to handle her mean mistress. And Mumbet knew her own worth and was scared of no one.

One day when the apple blossoms were in bloom, a shabbily dressed young girl appeared in the garden where Mumbet was hanging out the linen. The girl, eyes cast downward, asked to see Judge Ashley. The Judge was not at home, but Mumbet, knowing that the mistress would never want to see such a girl in her house, silently beckoned the child to come in. Then, looking about, she swiftly led her into the small bedroom off the kitchen and motioned for her to sit down on the bed. She shut the door behind her, hoping the mistress would not see, but as the door clicked shut, Mrs. Ashley met her in the hallway, her eyes flashing like a cat's.

Seeing no way to hide the child, Mumbet threw open the bedroom door, for she was determined to stand by her.

"What does *that* baggage want?" Mrs. Ashley demanded, pointing her finger at the unfortunate girl.

"To speak to Master," Mumbet replied calmly.

"What does *she* want to say to your master?"
Mrs. Ashley's eyes glinted dangerously.

Mumbet frowned back at her mistress, "I don't know ma'am."

"Get her out of here!" Mrs. Ashley bellowed, "She has no right to be in my house!"

Folding her arms across her chest, Mumbet took a deep breath. Turning to the girl she said, "You sit still, child."

Mrs. Ashley's face contorted with rage. "It's my house. Get her out!"

Gesturing to the girl, Mumbet repeated calmly, "Sit still, child."

"She shall go!"

Rising to her full height, Mumbet seemed to tower above her mistress. "No Missus, she shan't. If the girl has a complaint to make, she has a right to see the Judge; that's lawful, and stands to reason besides."

Mrs. Ashley stared at Mumbet. Knowing she could say nothing to this, she stomped off in a rage.

Mumbet stood for a full minute looking down the hall where her mistress had gone. Then she patted the tearful girl on the head and said, "Don't you worry. The Colonel will see you when he comes home. Mrs. Ashley knows that when I put my foot down, I keep it down."

When the Colonel arrived home that evening, Mumbet, holding a candle high, entered his study and said, "Sir, there is a young girl who has been waiting to see you all day. May I bring her in?"

"Waiting to see me? What about?"

"That's for her to tell."

"Bring her in."

The girl was shaking as Mumbet held her hand and led her in to see the Judge. Mumbet stood silently against the back wall as he questioned the child. Then, trusting that her master would be kind, she took the candle and left the room, shutting the door quietly behind her.

Later that night, Colonel Ashley spoke to Mumbet. "You did right by the child. She had a grievance that could not wait."

"Thank you, Sir."

Chapter 4

By 1773 the colonies had become a place of rebellion. All over, in the towns and in the countryside, people were talking heatedly about the high taxes they were forced to pay on tea and paper and other necessities. They were angry that they had to work for a king who lived so far away across the sea. They gathered along the roads and in taverns and homes. Colonel Ashley's upstairs study became an important meeting place for a committee of men working on a letter called a Declaration of Grievances to King George of England in the hope it would help America free itself from British rule. Eleven men, including Samuel Adams and Ethan Allen, met together for three days to draft this document. Colonel Ashley was the chairman of the committee and it was up to Mumbet to serve the gentleman tea, wait on them and clean up after them. She could not help but overhear their discussions.

"Massachusetts has always been a leader in matters such as this," said Samuel Adams. "We need to be leaders again! We long to be an independent country, able to make our own laws. Why should our tax money pay for the British army to stay here, as if we were children and couldn't take care of ourselves?"

"Everyone should have the right to be free!" agreed Ethan Allen.

"Freedom will come with a price, Ethan, and that price may be revolution!" said Colonel Ashley. "Are we ready for war?"

"I'd give my life to be rid of these troops!" harrumphed Mr. Allen. "They do us no service!"

"I wouldn't be so hot headed, Ethan, as to suggest violence! Let us make the law work for us!" replied Colonel Ashley.

"I would also prefer to stay this side of the law, Sir," added Aaron Root. "We have all been born equal and free, but the English Parliament obviously considers us unequal under the law! That is unacceptable."

The committee's clerk was a young man named Theodore Sedgwick, a lawyer from Sheffield who was often at the Ashley household speaking with the Colonel. He was well known to Mumbet and always treated her politely. He would come to be a very important person in her life.

As the gentlemen of the committee spoke, Mr. Sedgwick listened carefully and held his quill ready. After two days he wrote out the first sentence of what became known as the Sheffield Declaration: "Resolved that Mankind in a State of Nature are equal, free and independent of each other, and have a right to the undisturbed Enjoyment of their lives, Liberty and Property."

Mumbet, standing in the doorway, heard this talk of freedom and equality, listened to the men heatedly discuss their right to independence, and asked herself, "Why is it that I, who am not a beast, but am of Mankind, why is it that I cannot be free?" She thought about these words long after the men had returned to their homes.

As time went on, many of the colonists began preparing to fight. Often times on the village green there were speeches and discussions about equality, independence and freedom. Mumbet heard many of these speeches. She heard those stirring words over and over again, "All men are created free and equal." They excited her. She wondered what she could do to be a part of their meaning. If the country was fighting for freedom, wouldn't that mean freedom for everyone, including slaves?

Then, three years later, in 1776, America declared war on Britain. The War for Independence had begun. The town of Sheffield was in turmoil. Many husbands, brothers and fathers were going off to war. Each household prepared for its men-folk to join the army. Young and old, the men took up arms and prepared to fight for independence. Soon the town felt deserted with so many of the men gone off to war. The women had to do twice the work now. They banded together to support each other in doing the work the men had left behind, sometimes lending their servants, slaves and even their young sons to help with harvests and the heaviest chores. Each season seemed harder than the last.

A year later, a call came for new recruits. General Washington needed more soldiers to help fight the British. They began asking the enslaved men to join up and fight alongside the other soldiers. For this, the black soldiers were promised freedom at the end of the war in exchange for service. Mumbet's husband decided to join a local regiment.

"I'm joining up, Bet. When I get back, I'll be

a free man. And then I can work extra hard and buy you and Little Bet your precious freedom!"

Mumbet threw her arms around her husband, her heart full of his words. She knew it would be hard to have him gone, but wasn't the possibility of their own freedom worth the risk? She and Little Bet tearfully bade him farewell and with hope in his heart, he set off for war.

Late that summer, seven months after her husband had joined the army, Mumbet was kneeling in the garden digging the last of the potatoes. The sun was emerging from behind the clouds when she saw a neighbor, Azariah Root, striding purposefully up the path towards the Ashley kitchen door. He looked towards her as he passed and caught her eye. Something in his manner drew her attention. Gathering the basket of potatoes in her arms, she hurried towards the house only to overhear Squire Root already speaking to her master.

"John, I have some disturbing news."

Colonel Ashley looked at his friend. "What is it, neighbor? Pray tell me."

"I have had a letter from Colonel Paterson's unit," Squire Root continued. "A number of our men have been reported killed at the battle at Saratoga, among them is Bet's husband. I think it best that you should tell her."

With an agonized wail, Mumbet dropped the basket of potatoes. She held her hands to her ears trying to block out those words. They echoed in her head with finality. Without thinking she turned and ran towards the woods. She ran as fast as she could, the underbrush catching at her skirt, scratching her ankles, tripping her feet. She ran until she could run no more. The afternoon sun disappeared behind a dark cloud when she finally stumbled to the ground. Grief and shock consumed her and she wept uncontrollably. "Oh my love! Why?" she moaned, wiping her eyes, smearing dirt on her tear-streaked face.

What was to become of her? Of Little Bet? She thought of the smile she would never see again, his soft touch to her cheek. She thought of her daughter's joyous face when her daddy picked her up and put her high on his strong shoulders. She let out a wail of despair. The weight of her grief pulled her deeper towards the earth. She lay for a long time with her face in the grass. After what may have been hours, she felt the warm sun on her back. She turned towards it as it emerged from behind the clouds. The heat helped to soothe her sobs.

Mumbet stayed until the sun had sunk below the horizon, not concerned that the mistress might be wondering where she was. A chill had begun to rise up from the earth as she dragged herself to her feet. Standing still for a moment, she gazed about her. Everything looked the same, the trees, the fields, the path back to the house, but she knew her life had changed. She was now a widow. Her daughter had lost her father. Nothing would be the same. Reluctantly she turned back towards the house, looking for Little Bet. The evening star flickered in the sky. With swelling sorrow, Mumbet sighed and said aloud, "It must be God's will."

Throughout the fall and winter she and Little Bet did their work with little thought for anything but their grief. For a short while, Mrs. Ashley was lenient and didn't push them to work harder. Mumbet somberly realized that in losing her husband, she most certainly had lost her chance to be free.

Chapter 5

The war dragged on. News from the colonies was not encouraging and the townsfolk began to worry that their husbands, brothers and fathers would never return. The women talked gloomily among themselves, while sewing quilts, weaving blankets and knitting socks for the soldiers. They knew their men were suffering from the cold and wet, from the long marches and poor food. There was not much they could do except send them supplies and wait for their return.

One day, several years into the war, Mrs. Ashley seemed to be in a worse mood than ever before. A young servant girl had taken some leftover scraps of cornmeal to make herself a little corn cake. When Mrs. Ashley found out about this, she stormed into the kitchen.

"You thief! How dare you steal from my larder! You'll not steal again or I know what!" Mrs. Ashley sputtered.

Mumbet heard the uproar in the kitchen and came running in, just in time to see Mrs. Ashley grab a red-hot shovel from the hearth. The mistress lifted the shovel and was about to strike the young girl, when Mumbet put her own arm up to block the blow and was struck instead. Her arm was burned to the bone. It burned and burned. And so did her outrage. This time Mrs. Ashley had gone too far. Mumbet never covered her wound. She wanted everyone to know what had happened. When visitors to the house saw the scar, they often said, "Why Betty, what ails your arm?"

Mumbet's answer was simply, "Ask Madame."

From then on, Mumbet knew she could no longer tolerate such a life but did not know what to do. The answer came in 1780 with the writing

of the Massachusetts Constitution. This was an important document that expressed the rights and responsibilities of all the citizens of Massachusetts. It was so vital, that the leaders in Boston sent messengers on horseback to each town to read it to the citizens. One evening, a messenger arrived in Sheffield to read it to the townsfolk. Mumbet went with her daughter to hear it read on the Sheffield green. Again she heard those stirring words: "All men are born free and equal..." Realizing it was a new law, not just a letter to the King, she grew excited and asked herself, "How can I make this law work for *me*?" She hurried back with her daughter, thinking the whole way.

Bet could think of nothing else as the days passed. She thought of freedom as she made the meals and polished the silver.

She thought of it as she boiled the linen and stoked the fires.

She dreamed of it at night as she lay on her bed of straw.

She imagined what it would be like to do as she pleased, to be accountable to no one but herself. She smiled at the thought. Throughout the winter, the idea of freedom was in her mind. It would not leave.

Spring came. Her arm was finally healed. She looked down at the scar and felt suddenly her time had come. She must be free. She realized that there was only one thing to do, she must go to a lawyer and put this law to work. To arouse no suspicion, she waited until the next market day, and with her basket over her arm, she and Little Bet walked four miles into the town of Sheffield to the home of Theodore Sedgwick, the young lawyer she had come to know over the years.

When she was shown into his study he appeared startled and said, "Why Betty, what brings you here?"

"Mr. Sedgwick," she replied, "I've come to ask

if you could help me win my freedom in a court
of law."

Mr. Sedgwick was taken aback. "Why, what
put such notions into your head, Betty?"

"I heard that gentleman talking on the green
about the new laws in the land and I believe that
I can be a part of that freedom."

"And what would you base your suit on?"

"I heard what you talked on before and I heard those papers that were read in the study. That every man is born free and equal. Does that not stand for women too, and slaves at that? Must I really be a slave in Massachusetts? I'm not a dumb critter, Mr. Sedgwick, and I am certainly one of the Nation. My own dear husband gave his life to help free this land! Don't you know that?"

"I did know, Betty, and for that I am sorry. But my question to you is, how did you come to know of this?"

"By keepin' still and minding things," she replied.

Chapter 6

Mumbet took her daughter out into the garden while Mr. Sedgwick sat alone at his desk thinking long and hard about what she had said. He agreed that there was an illogic to slavery at a time when the country was fighting for freedom. And, he thought, if there was a possibility of winning this case, didn't he have a responsibility to take it on? Then he carefully pondered the consequences of suing his good friend, Colonel Ashley. Finally, he came to the conclusion that, friend or not, Mumbet had a right to be heard in a court of law.

He decided to take Mumbet's case. He called her back into his study.

"Bet, I want to help you. I think we can make a case. But you will have to find a man to bring suit along with you, because," he reminded her, "as a woman, you have no rights in court."

Mumbet thanked Mr. Sedgwick, and said, "Perhaps my friend Brom will want to be a free man; maybe he will join me on this case."

Full of hope, she took Little Bet by the hand, went to market and returned to the home of Colonel Ashley. It was the last place she wanted to be and although Mumbet had often thought about running away and had heard about slaves who had, she wanted to be freed in a lawful way.

She wanted to sue for her freedom in a court of law and put the nation's new justice system to work.

That night, under cover of darkness, she slipped outside and found Brom down by the river where he liked to sit and smoke his pipe.

"Bet, what are you doin' here so late at night?" Brom asked, startled.

Bet sat down on a log across from him and

closed her eyes for a moment. When she opened them, Brom could tell she was excited about something.

"Brom, I've been listening to what those men are saying in the study when I cater to them, about freedom. Well, there's a law now says as how all men are free. I want that law to work for me."

"You ain't no man, Bet. You a slave like me."

"But Brom, we don't have to be. Mr. Sedgwick told me so. He agreed to take my case. I'm gonna sue for my freedom. He told me to ask you to sue along with me. I got no rights as a woman, but you do as a man, and together, we might be able to get free of this bondage."

"My life ain't so bad, Bet. Got my pipe when my work's done. Got a place to lay my head.

Where would I go?"

"I know you got all that, as do I. But do they pay us for our labor? Can you leave if you want? And I know the Colonel's son don't treat you too good. As for the mistress..." she held out her scarred arm to Brom.

Brom nodded his head in agreement. Colonel Ashley's son was General Ashley. He owned Brom. And everyone said it was too bad that he took after his mother. Brom had been beaten on several occasions.

Bet put her hands on Brom's broad shoulders and looked him in the eye.

"Brom, Mr. Sedgwick is a good man, and a good lawyer. Let him get us both our freedom. I can't do it without you."

It was a plea, and Brom heard it in her voice.

He never knew Bet to beg for anything and he realized how much this meant to her. Her dream of freedom hadn't died with her husband. Brom remembered Bet helping him soothe his wounds in the dark of night after a particularly brutal whipping. He sat back against the tree and pulled deeply on his pipe. Bet watched the smoke swirl out from his mouth and up into the starlit sky. She said a silent prayer on the smoke and waited for Brom to reply.

"I'm gonna help you Bet. Being a free man sounds good. Real good."

Mumbet had no words; her heart was so full of hope and gratitude. Through tears of joy, she smiled at Brom, squeezed his shoulder and left him to his thoughts.

Mumbet gazed up at the night sky and saw

the evening star twinkling as she made her way
back to her bed.

Chapter 7

Two days later, Mr. Sedgwick issued a "writ of replevin" to Colonel Ashley. This was an order to take back stolen goods and property. The property in question was two people, Mumbet and Brom, who were declared as being held illegally.

Two sheriffs arrived at Colonel Ashley's house demanding that he release Mumbet, stating that she was being held unlawfully.

"Colonel Ashley," one of the sheriffs said, "We are here with this writ demanding you release one slave named Bet."

"What is the meaning of this!" Colonel Ashley was outraged.

"John, what is all this commotion?" Hannah Ashley demanded, coming down the stairs in her dressing gown.

"Go back upstairs, Hannah, I will deal with this."

Mumbet stood behind the kitchen door

watching and listening. At that moment, her heart soared because she knew Mr. Sedgwick was making good his promise.

Colonel Ashley was shocked. He knew these sheriffs. He felt betrayed by the woman who had lived in his home all these years.

"Bet!"

Mumbet walked purposefully from out of the kitchen.

"Bet, did you bring these allegations against me?"

"I did, Sir."

"But you are my servant, Bet, we need you here. This is nonsense. You may not leave."

"Master, I am not your servant, I am your *slave* and as such have no freedom."

Hannah, making no move to return upstairs, raised her voice and shouted down, "How dare you, you ungrateful wretch!"

"Hannah! Please!" Turning back to Bet, Colonel Ashley spoke again, "You are my servant, Bet. I have never treated you harshly nor have I made extraordinary demands of you! Don't you have enough to eat? A warm place to sleep?"

"But Master," Mumbet said, holding up her arm, "I want my freedom. I have a right to it. I am not a beast. I am of mankind. The law says all men are free and equal."

Colonel Ashley could not argue with what Bet said. His own work on the Sheffield Declaration had contributed to the thoughts expressed in the Massachusetts Constitution. Yet he refused to release Mumbet from bondage, claiming that if he were to give up Mumbet, *his* property, he would have to be given a bond, some security that if she were not to win her case she would be returned to him. He sent the sheriffs away empty handed.

That same night, a second writ was delivered to Colonel Ashley's son, the General, for Brom, who was suing alongside Mumbet. The General also refused to release his slave, arguing that the man had been lawfully purchased.

Theodore Sedgwick was not surprised by these events and ordered a new writ of replevin. A few days later, on June 5, the sheriffs arrived at the

Ashley house with another writ as well as a bond.
The Colonel had no choice but to accept matters
as they stood. He watched as Mumbet gathered
her daughter and their few possessions and
stepped out of his house, perhaps never to return.
Mumbet looked once more at the house that had

been her home for over thirty years. She would miss Selah and the herb garden and nights under the stars singing with her fellows. But freedom came with a price.

Mumbet and her daughter walked to the Sedgwick home in Sheffield where she had been offered a place in their household while waiting for the case to be tried. In return, she would help them with their three young children—Eliza, Frances and Theodore.

Brom promised his master, the General, he would continue to work for him until the case was settled, for he had nowhere else to go.

Chapter 8

Theodore Sedgwick consulted Tapping Reeve, an older and more experienced lawyer from Sharon, Connecticut. The two would work together to prepare for the trial. The case was called Brom and Bet vs. Ashley. There was a buzz of excitement in Sheffield and Great Barrington as the lawsuit was prepared over the summer. Was this a way to see if all slaves could be made free?

How could it be legal to have slaves when the country was fighting a war for freedom, independence and equality?

Colonel Ashley also hired the best legal counsel he could find. Jonathan Canfield from Connecticut and David Noble from Williamstown agreed to represent Colonel Ashley in court. Mrs. Ashley repeatedly demanded they do something about "*her* runaway slave!"

On August 19, 1781 Theodore Sedgwick, Tapping Reeve, Mumbet and Brom arrived at the courthouse in Great Barrington ready to take on the cause of freedom. Colonel Ashley and his lawyers arrived too, amidst much clamor. The crowd surged around them as they entered the courthouse. Everyone wanted to hear what the lawyers would argue.

Colonel Ashley's lawyers went first. They argued that "... Brom and Bet, are and were at the time of the original writ, the legal Negro servants of the said John Ashley during their lives." They said that this could be proven and the case should be dropped.

Sedgwick and Reeve came next. They argued that Brom and Bet were not the legal servants of John Ashley during their lives and that there was no law in Massachusetts that clearly established slavery in the first place. They stated that even if there were laws allowing slavery, the new Massachusetts Constitution would revoke those laws. All men were free in Massachusetts.

The trial lasted only two days. That day and the next, the jury heard more of the case and at the end of those two days both judge and jury were convinced. On August 21, 1781, it was found that "Brom and Bet are not and were not at the time of the purchase of the original Writ the legal Negro Servants of him the said John Ashley during life."

There was a stunned silence in the court. A huge collective sigh breathed through the room as everyone realized what had just occurred. In the loud cheering that erupted, no one heard Mumbet's words, "I am *free.*" She repeated them three times. Looking around, she grabbed Little Bet by the hand and strode purposefully out of the courtroom onto the grass under the blazing August sun and repeated, "I am *free!*" She tasted the words on her tongue and turned to her daughter and said, "We are free!"

She stood there dazedly. Thirty-seven years of servitude. Over. She was a free woman. People spilled out of the courthouse, congratulating each other, some stopping to congratulate her and Brom. Bet had no words for them but her eyes were shining. She felt Brom standing near her. She turned to look at him, searching his face for his thoughts. Tears were welling in his eyes. Suddenly she was weeping. She held her hands up to her face, trying to hide her tears. Brom put his arm around her shoulder. "There, there. Hush now, hush." She rested her head on his chest, crying quietly for a few moments. Drying her eyes with her handkerchief, she looked up at him. "We are free, Brom," she whispered, "We are free!"

Brom nodded at her, his eyes full of joy, "We are. And it feels real good!"

As the crowd milled around, Mumbet and Brom stood next to each other, seeing everything with new eyes. Tapping Reeve made his way out of the courthouse. Seeing Mumbet and Brom, he walked over, smiling broadly, hand outstretched. Brom took it.

"What are you going to do now, Brom?" he asked, "Will you be going back to the General's?"

Brom looked gratefully at the man who had helped to free him. "I ain't got no where else to go, Sir. But things will be different. I can stay there and work as long as I need to, but now, I can leave if I want. It's what's best."

Bet knew there were not many choices for them now, even free.

"Good man. Congratulations to you both." He tipped his hat and walked away.

The crowd had thinned. Bet squeezed Brom's arm as she saw Colonel Ashley making his way towards them.

"Bet, you have your precious freedom!" Colonel Ashley said, "Would you consider staying on with us? We would pay you a wage, of course."

"Mr. Ashley," she replied, no longer referring to him as *master,* "I have been offered a position with the Sedgwicks. I know the children now and their household ways. They need me. Little Bet and I are happy there."

Colonel Ashley stood looking at Mumbet for a few silent moments then turned on his heel and walked away.

Not only were Mumbet and Brom declared free, but Colonel Ashley had been ordered to pay 30 shillings in damages as well as all court costs, which were five pounds, fourteen shillings, and four pence lawful money. The new law had worked.

Few realized at that moment what a profound and far-reaching effect this case would have on all the slaves in Massachusetts in the years to come.

Chapter 9

That fall was one of the most beautiful in memory. The asters and the goldenrod bloomed purple and yellow along the field edges. The world seemed full of life and color. Every day was a wonder to Bet and she felt contented and happy for the first time. She proudly took the name of "Elizabeth Freeman" but was still known affectionately as Mumbet. Theodore Sedgwick was building up his practice as a lawyer and a politician. There were three little children to take care of. There was another baby on the way. The days were still long and there was much work to be done, but she and Little Bet were free to come and go as they pleased. They shared a room and Little Bet, who was eleven at the time, helped her mother care for the young children.

Mumbet was there by Pamela Sedgwick's side when she gave birth to her son. She encouraged and comforted her as she delivered the baby. Her skill as nurse and midwife improved with each delivery and she was often called out to attend to a birth. Although she worked for the Sedgwicks, they never complained when she set out with her baskets of herbs and poultices to deliver neighboring babies. As Mumbet's reputation grew, she prided herself on the fact that she never lost a baby in the birthing.

Mumbet kept her midwifery fees in the leather drawstring herb sack her mother had given her. Whenever she deposited money in her little "bank" she smelled those herbs and thought of her mother. She was saving her money for something special.

Theodore Sedgwick had been elected to the General Court in Boston and spent much time

away from home. Mumbet kept Mrs. Sedgwick and the children company during those lonely times. The trip to Boston could take up to a week, so Mr. Sedgwick was often gone for months at a time. There were many new laws being introduced and Mr. Sedgwick had a part in the writing of those laws. He loved his time in Boston. He was an ambitious man and sought out the prestige that went along with being a member of the court.

Mumbet's workload was lightened when two years later Agrippa Hull and his wife Jane Darby, joined the household. Agrippa was a free black man, newly returned from serving six years in the American army under the famous Polish general Thaddeus Kosciuszko.

A few years later, in 1783, Theodore Sedgwick decided to move his family to Stockbridge, a town twelve miles north of Sheffield. He bought the last remaining piece of land owned on the main street by a Native Mahican, a woman called Elizabeth Pewauwyausquauh-Wanwianyrequenot. She had lived in a wigwam on this land her whole life. Now, as the last of the Stockbridge Mahican Indians were moved to a reservation in Oneida, New York, she felt she too had to sell her land. She sold this piece, which overlooked the Housatonic River, for 30 pounds lawful money to

Theodore Sedgwick and moved away with the rest of her tribe.

Theodore had big plans for this land. He wanted to build the finest house in Stockbridge and he himself designed his dream house. It took almost three years to build but when it was finished in 1785 it was a mansion with tall ceilings and windows, and many, many rooms. It was easily twice as big as their house in Sheffield. Just before they moved, Pamela Sedgwick gave birth to a son, Henry Dwight. The growing Sedgwick family, including Mumbet and Little Bet, all happily moved to the grand new house.

"Mammy Bet! Look at these tall windows! I can see for miles!" cried ten-year-old Eliza in delight.

Little Frannie, running up the wide staircase, opening every door, called out, "There's a fireplace in every room!" Mumbet smiled at the children, thinking about the cleaning of those windows and

the building of those fires in the many hearths,
but she did not spoil the girls' pleasure. It was a
beautiful home and Mumbet was glad for the
opportunity to live in such a grand house. Agrippa
and Jane moved into their own little house nearby
on Goodrich Lane, continuing to work in the
household.

As fall turned to winter, Samson, a runaway slave, joined the household and became their cook. He never talked about where he had come from or where he had learned to cook, but everyone was pleased by his culinary skills, including Mumbet, who had enough to do. Moses Orcutt joined the staff soon after, doing all the heavy work. This gave Mumbet more time to devote to caring for the four young children and continue her nursing among the townsfolk.

In 1783 a treaty was signed between Britain and the Colonies. The Revolutionary War was over. America was free from British rule. The soldiers returned home but, upon their return, many of them found they were being required to pay higher taxes than before the war.

Before the war, they had been allowed to barter their taxes for a sack of potatoes or a peck of wheat, but now the government was demanding cash to pay these taxes. Here they had been gone for years at a time, unable to work on their farms and now they were expected to come up with real money. If they could not pay the taxes, they were often sent to jail and their land taken from them. Most of the soldiers were farmers and had been unable to sow their fields and grow their crops and so had nothing to sell and no money. Their wives had struggled to make ends meet during the war and now their husbands were being arrested for something that was beyond their control.

For a time the soldiers stated their grievances in an orderly fashion. But the people in the government ignored them at every turn. The soldiers became angry and frustrated that after years of service in the army, it seemed as if they were being punished for helping their country win the war!

In response to this situation, some of the former soldiers banded together and started a rebellion. The man in charge was called Daniel Shays. These men wanted to take revenge on the local representatives of government and business. Theodore Sedgwick was a perfect target.

For weeks Mumbet and the family heard tell of a group of angry soldiers who, in their frustration, had decided to take the law into their own hands. They were making their way towards

Stockbridge, fighting whoever had the misfortune to get in their way. The Sedgwicks knew without a doubt that their destination would be the family home. Since Theodore Sedgwick had to be in Boston as part of his work, he sent his wife and children, along with Little Bet, to stay at the home of a friend, in case the dissenters attacked his home.

He left only Mumbet and the other servants to protect the house from the would-be invaders. He knew, if anyone could protect his home, they could.

The next day a neighbor came over to tell Mumbet that the soldiers were within a few miles of Stockbridge. Although she was sympathetic to their grievances, she knew they were angry and set on revenge. She didn't want them to find anything of value to destroy, so she gathered together the Sedgwicks' silver and jewels, put them into bags, and hurriedly brought them to her attic room and placed them in her own wooden chest. She then went down into the cellar and covered the barrels of good wine with heavy cloth and pushed a barrel of old beer towards the bottom of the stairs. She would be ready to protect the household, if necessary.

With the family gone, Mumbet kept only the kitchen fire burning for warmth as well as for cooking. After a hurried supper, she settled herself down on the hearth and fell into a fitful sleep, not knowing if or when they would be coming.

Before long, a loud banging was heard at the front door. Waking with a start and jumping to her feet, Mumbet hurried to the door armed with a long handled shovel.

She stood in the hallway, bracing herself. She heard the men calling loudly. Their leader banged his gun against the door once more.

"Open up! Come out Squire Sedgwick, you coward!"

Mumbet squared her shoulders, took a deep breath and opened the door, glaring at the men. She held the shovel in front of her.

"What are you doing banging your gun against my door?" she demanded.

"*Your* door? This is the home of Theodore Sedgwick."

"We have a knocker. You would be smart to use it," she said, admonishing them.

"Bring him to us! Bring us Sedgwick!"

"*Mr.* Sedgwick is not here."

"We'll see about that. Now stand aside or we'll push you aside."

Mumbet looked at the men. Some of their faces looked familiar. She recognized Sam Cooper, who had been selling his brooms only the week before. Mumbet had bought two of them to help his family. She gave him a hard look.

"What are you doing here, Sam Cooper? Why aren't you home with those children of yours?"

Sam Cooper looked at his feet. "We're here for a reason, Mumbet. We've got real grievances!"

"I know the reason, but destroying this house is not going to get you the justice you want."

"You'd better move aside, wench! We're going to search this house!" one of the other men yelled.

She knew that whatever they were looking for, they would not find, and she moved out of their way.

"Come in and search. You'll not find anything here."

Mumbet led the men through the front parlor, the dining room, and the kitchen. She watched in disgust as they tramped their boots over her polished floors and up the stairs to the bedrooms, thrusting their bayonets under the beds and in the bedding in search of Theodore Sedgwick. Finding no man, nor any guns or silver, they tromped down to the cellar and discovered the keg of beer she had placed strategically for them. One of them opened it and took a swig, only to spit it out, for it was sour.

"What foul drink is this?"

"It's what the gentlemen like. You must not be gentlemen, then," Mumbet said, mockingly.

They kicked the beer barrel aside and went back upstairs, grumbling all the way. Seeing that they had been in all the bedrooms, they found the stairs to the attic and ran up them sure they would find something.

Their eyes lit up when they saw Mumbet's padlocked trunk. "Get us the key, wench!" one of the men demanded.

Mumbet was irate. "You and your fellows are no better than I thought you. You call me "wench" and you are not above rummaging in my chest. You'll have to break it open to do so. While you're at it, why not look under my bed! Poke around my clothes! Maybe you'll find some guns or even the Squire!"

Put in their place, the men sheepishly turned and went back downstairs. Mumbet sat on her wooden chest, her heart pounding, until the last man left the room.

Then she followed them to the front door. Sam Cooper tipped his hat to her. "Thank you, Ma'am Bet."

She nodded her head, bolting the door behind her. She took a breath and let it out, hard. "Lord have mercy!" she whispered. "By God's grace we are safe!"

Chapter 10

"Come quickly, Mumbet!" Jane Darby cried from the landing, her anxious face leaning over the banister. Mumbet got up from stoking the fire in the kitchen, wiped her hands on her apron and ran up the wide stairs.

Jane took her arm and led her into Pamela Sedgwick's bedroom where the woman was bent over in pain.

"Betty, the baby's coming and it's too early!" groaned Pamela.

"Hush now, Madame, come over here to the bed and lie down."

Mumbet gently rubbed Pamela's back and led her to the bed, quieting and calming her.

"Please help me, Betty. What's wrong?"

"It seems this little one wants to come now and can't wait for her birthday time. Breathe, Madame. Just breathe."

Mumbet examined the frightened woman and realized that the baby really was coming, some two months early and there was nothing anyone could do about it, except hope for the best.

"Jane, can you stoke up the fire in here and call Little Bet? I need hot water and clean linens."

"Of course."

It was only three days after Christmas and bitterly cold. The house was still decorated

festively. The children were playing in the nursery with nineteen-year-old Little Bet, far away from the cries of their mother. Theodore Sedgwick was downstairs in his office, busily preparing papers to take to Boston.

"Little Bet, run and get me my herbs," Mumbet instructed her daughter. She knew just what to give Mrs. Sedgwick to take the edge off the pain and get her ready for the birthing.

Late that night, Theodore came up the stairs to find his wife holding their new, tiny daughter. They named her Catharine Maria. Pamela smiled at her husband, but this birth had weakened her and it was difficult for her to care for the infant. Mumbet took the baby under her care and loved her like her own daughter.

Mrs. Sedgwick recovered slowly but never regained her strength. Catharine, tiny as she was, gradually grew strong and robust under Mumbet's care.

One day, as Mumbet was bouncing Catharine on her knee, Little Bet came up behind her mother, her face wreathed in smiles.

"Mama!" she spoke breathlessly, "I have something to tell you! Jonah has asked me to marry him and I said yes!"

Mumbet turned towards her daughter, her face beaming, "Oh child, that is good news indeed!"

Jonah Humphrey had been courting Little Bet for almost a year. Spring was coming up on summer, and it was a good time to get married. Jonah owned a house near Agrippa and Jane on Cherry Hill. Jonah planted a garden and put the finishing touches on their new home before his bride moved in. Many friends came to the wedding party and what a party it was! Catered by Agrippa

and Jane, the food was tasty and plentiful. There was dancing and music and Mumbet beamed with delight, knowing her daughter would be happy and close by.

Within a year, Mumbet held her first grandchild in her arms. Although Mumbet continued living with the Sedgwicks she spent much of her time with her new grandbaby, often bringing her to play with little Catharine.

Mumbet took great pride in watching Catharine grow up. Catharine was a natural-born storyteller, and, of all the people in her life, Catharine chose Mumbet to share her many stories with. She loved listening to the girl.

"Catharine, you weave a fine tale! You should write those stories down."

"Mammy Bet, I think I might do that!"

Mumbet remained at the Sedgwicks for the next ten years. She had raised all the Sedgwick children. They loved her like a mother.

After Pamela Sedgwick passed away and when Catharine was grown, Mumbet realized that the family no longer needed her. She had raised them well. Her own growing family wanted her to be near them as she aged. She added up her savings from her little bank and knew what she would use her money for. She had spied a piece of land on Agawam Pond, near her daughter and dreamed of a house there. With her earnings she was able to buy twelve acres of land and build a small home for herself in the middle of the new and growing community of free blacks. It was a day filled with pride when she moved into her very own home, a free and independent woman. She saw her grandchildren and great-grandchildren often and happily spoiled and indulged them. There she lived for the next twenty-two years, continuing to serve both the black and white communities as nurse and midwife. Her skills, wit and wisdom were much sought after.

She planted a garden and filled it with herbs. She often lingered there, amongst the sweet-smelling flowers, and looked up at the night sky, looking for the evening star, her mother's star.

Catharine visited her "Mammy Bet" whenever she was in town, and for one of Mumbet's birthdays, Catharine gave her a gold beaded necklace, which Mumbet wore always.

She loved to sit on her porch rocker surrounded by her grandchildren and great-grandchildren and tell them about her life as a slave and then as a free woman. Many times, her eyes misting over, she would say these words:

"Any time, any time when I was a slave, if I had been offered one minute's freedom and told that at the end of that minute I would have to die, I would have taken it, just to stand one minute a free woman on God's earth, I would."

The children looked at her proudly, knowing that because of her, they too were free. "Oh, Granny Bet, you've had more than one minute of freedom!"

"Yes, I've been a free woman on God's earth for near fifty years."

Epilogue
1829

This is a true story. Mumbet lived and died a folk hero and legend in her time. The reason we know so much about Mumbet's life is that Catharine Sedgwick did indeed become a famous storywriter. She was one of the first women novelists in America. She loved to tell stories about Mumbet. She visited Mumbet whenever she could. On Catharine's fortieth birthday, December 28, 1829 Mumbet died at the supposed age of eighty-five. Catharine was there by her side. She describes the scene in her book *The Power of Her Sympathy*: "I do not believe that any amount of temptation could have induced Mumbet to swerve from the truth. She knew nothing of the compromises of timidity, or the overwrought consciousness of bigotry. Truth was her nature—the offspring of courage—truth and loyalty. In my childhood I clung to her with instinctive love and faith, and the more I know and observe of human nature, the higher does she rise above others, whatever may have been their instruction or accomplishment. In her the image of her Maker was cast in material so hard and pure that circumstances could not alter its outline or cloud its luster... I well remember that during her last sickness, when I daily visited her in her little hut— her then independent home—I said then, and my sober after-judgment ratified it, that I felt awed as if I had entered the presence of [George] Washington. Even protracted suffering and mortal sickness and old age, could not break down her spirit."

Mumbet is buried in the Stockbridge, Massachusetts cemetery in what is affectionatley known as "The Sedgwick Family Pie," next to Catharine Sedgwick. Her headstone reads:

Elizabeth Freeman

known by the name of

MUMBET

died Dec. 28, 1829
Her supposed age
was 85 years

She was born a slave and remained a slave for nearly thirty years. She could neither read nor write, yet in her own sphere she had no superior nor equal. She neither wasted time nor property. She never violated a truth, nor failed to perform a duty. In every situation of domestic trial, she was the most efficient helper and the tenderest friend. Good mother, farewell.

She is the only non-family member to be buried there. And her legacy lives on.

Historical Context

According to historical records the first ship to arrive in America with enslaved African men and women on board arrived at Jamestown, Virginia in 1619. This was one year before the Pilgrims landed on Plimoth Rock in Massachusetts. These people had been stolen from Africa and brought to America to help the early colonists with the hard work of tilling the land and building houses and fortifications in this unknown and wild country. From then on, enslaved African people worked for their "owners" for over two hundred years, until the end of the Civil War in 1865.

In 1829 when Mumbet died, dehumanizing and brutal laws continued to enslave Africans who lived in America. In most of the other states the slaves were not free. There were laws that controlled almost every aspect of their lives. But, in Massachusetts they had already been free for 46 years. This was due, in part, to the courage of Mumbet. In having the bravery to sue for her freedom, in speaking what was in her heart, she changed the course of history, thereby setting the stage for the rest of the slaves in Massachusetts to be freed. In 1783, two years after Mumbet gained her freedom in the Great Barrington court of law, all the other approximately 3,000 slaves who lived in Massachusetts at that time were set free. This was based on Mumbet's case and one other called the Quok Walker case. Slavery was banned by judicial decree (in a court of law). Chief Justice William Cushing in his ruling, declared: "The idea of slavery is inconsistent with our own conduct and the Constitution; and there can be no such thing as perpetual servitude of a rational creature."

Although the burden of obtaining their freedom was placed on each individual slave, they at least had this option. By the 1790 census, there were no more slaves *listed* in Massachusetts. This was 80 years before America fought its Civil War which freed all the slaves. Even after the Civil War was over, life for the freed slaves was not easy. Evil and degrading laws and customs still limited and constrained their lives. But that is content for our next story.

It has been (erroneously) written in a variety of places that Mumbet was the first slave to sue for her freedom. Unfortunately, this is *inexcusably* misleading. Slaves had been successfully suing for their freedom in Massachusetts since 1701. But they sued based on the premise of a broken promise, such as "you promised I would be free when I was 21" or "I was promised my freedom upon the death of my owner." And slaves had been *negotiating* for their freedom from the time the first slave ships arrived on American shores in the early 1600s. What made Mumbet's suit for freedom so different was that she sued based on a new law: Article 1 of the Bill of Rights of the Massachusetts Constitution. She was by far not the first to sue; simply she was the first to sue on the premise that "all men are created free and equal." And that is what makes this story so special. In putting the laws of the nation to work for her, she helped free the other slaves in Massachusetts.

Dear Reader,

You may be wondering how we got all this information about Mumbet. Since she was a folk-hero in her town during her lifetime, many different stories have been told about her, some true, some close to the truth and others just plain made up. You may have heard stories about Mumbet that are different from ours. Many people mention Mumbet's "sister", Lizzie, but we have not included her in our story because that would have meant that Mumbet's mother would have named both of her children "Elizabeth" (Bet and Lizzie) and we don't think she would have done that. Also, there is no mention of Lizzie in any written documents, including Mumbet's will.

We have gathered our information from a variety of sources over many years. These include books by Catharine Maria Sedgwick; John

Sedgwick (Catharine's great-great-great-great-great-great nephew); Mumbet's own last will and testament, which is at the courthouse in Pittsfield, Massachusetts and available to anyone; articles by Arthur Silversmit, who wrote scholarly pieces on Mumbet; Mary Wilds' *Mumbet, The Life and Times of Elizabeth Freeman* and many old books written in the 1800s.

To learn about life as it was at the time when Mumbet lived we referred to the many articles at the Sheffield Historical Society; James Miller's *Early Life in Sheffield, Massachusetts* and *Sheffield, Frontier Town* by Lillian Price; *If They Close the Door on You, Go in the Window* by Bernard Drew and *"Friends of Liberty"* by Gary Nash & Graham Russel Gao Hodges. We will use these resources again in our next books.

We spent countless hours at the Ashley House where Mumbet spent so many years as a slave, at the Sheffield Historical Society researching whatever we could find about life back then, and also visited the Sedgwick House. Our favorite place was Mumbet's grave in Stockbridge where we tried to commune with her spirit. We hope she is as proud of this book as we are.

The Authors

Acknowledgments

Special thanks must be given to all the people who helped us with the creation, writing and birthing of this book. They are:

Lisa Anderson, formerly of The Trustees of Reservations, who unwittingly and graciously set us on the path, Zufan (our model) and the Bazzano Family; Jonathan Barnes, Joy Bergins, Sara Ciborski, Richard Courage, Dianna Downing, Shawnee Barnes-Emmett, James Ferris, Kat Goddard, Robin Goldberg, Amira Barnes Gundel, Wray Gunn, Emma Hulbert, Frances Jones-Sneed, Christine Kelley and her 2nd graders from Undermountain Elementary School, Zoë Laiz, E.B. Lewis, Kim Lorang, Martin Meader, Patty Melville, Richard Meyers, Elizabeth Neale, Kate Pichard, Cora Portnoff, Christina M. Root, Nancy & John Root, Sr., Kaitlin Scarbro and her 3rd graders from Muddy Brook Elementary School, Jodi Schuyten, John Sedgwick, Arthur Schwartz, Millie Tennenbaum, Nancy Tunnicliffe, Alec Walling, Claudette Webster, and Rene Wendell.

JL, AEB, JR

Praise for "*A Free Woman on God's Earth*"

"Born a slave, but freed by my ancestor Theodore Sedgwick, Mumbet came to work for the family as a paid servant, and quickly found her way into the hearts of those first Sedgwicks, and through them to their descendants and now out to the wider world. With her soulful pride and majestic grace, Mumbet is a woman of lovely paradox. Ann-Elizabeth Barnes and Jana Laiz have captured that and more in this lively and moving account of Mumbet's impressive life, a book that is sure to bring yet another generation of readers and citizens into the thrall of this great American heroine."

John Sedgwick, New York Times bestselling author of
*In My Blood, Six Generations of Madness and Desire in an
American Family*

"*A Free Woman on God's Earth*" by Jana Laiz and Ann-Elizabeth Barnes is a beautifully told history of one of the bravest women to grace the American landscape. Told with sensitivity and love, this story will have children wanting to learn more about the unsung heroes and heroines who shaped the course of history. Not just a book about slavery, "*A Free Woman on God's Earth*" is about the power of one voice and the triumph of the human spirit. I highly recommend this book for children and teachers."

Martin Meader, Author of *The Adventures of Charlie
& Moon* and The Co-Executive Producer/Co-Story Writer
Paradise Ro

"This is a story of a brave, courageous woman who made a difference in the lives of enslaved blacks and women in the 18th century. Elizabeth "Mumbet" Freeman is clearly a role model for all Americans in this difficult time. The writers present a clear, easy-to-read narrative that is written in an engaging style that will hold our interest and make us want to stand up and take action to address the inequalities that still exist in our own communities."

Frances Jones-Sneed, Ph.D. Professor of History & Director of Women Studies, Massachusetts College of Liberal Arts

"...a fascinating presentation on the facts of Mumbet's life. ...easy to read with the story line presented in a straight forward way. ...exciting passages that I reread a second time ..."

Wray Gunn , Trustee African American Heritage Trail and AME Zion Church

"A wonderful account of Mumbet, the Ashley family, Theodore Sedgwick and the others involved in her historical and successful bid for freedom in Massachusetts. It is an engrossing story written with wonderful detail and conversations that sweep the reader into Mumbet's life and trials. Even if you feel you know your history, you will find some new aspects here to keep you engaged. The writing is smooth, detailed and absorbing. Good reading for the young and the not so young as well."

Cora Portnoff, Trustee African American Heritage Trail